BE PATIENT,

BE BRAVE, FEARLESS, NEVER IN A HASTE

KEITH PAUL PHILLIP

North Vertical LLC
northverticali8@gmail.com
(347) 548-7937

Table of Contents

Not even if you call an eye a nose and a nose an eye.

Blind in one nose, deaf in one eye.

Lead is heavier than sand.

Light as a feather, or as heavy a lead, we need justice.

Psalm 139

Jah, you have searched me and, known me. You know my sitting down and my rising up. You understand my thoughts afar off. You comprehend my path and my lying down and are acquainted with all my ways. For there is not a word on my tongue, but behold, oh Jah, you know it altogether. You have hedged me behind and before and laid your hand upon me. Such knowledge is too wonderful for me, it is high I cannot attain it. Where can I go from your spirit? Or where can I flee from your presence? If I ascend into heaven, you are there. If I make my bed in hell, behold, you are there. If I take the wings of the morning and dwell in the uttermost part of the sea, even there your hands shall lead me and your right hand shall hold me. If I say, "Surely, the darkness shall fall be light about me." Indeed, the darkness shall not hide from you. For you formed my inward parts, you covered me in my mother's womb. I will praise you, for I am fearfully and wonderfully made. Marvelous are your works and that my soul know very well. My fram was not hidden from you when I was made in secret, and skillfully wrought in the lowest part of the earth. Your eyes saw my substance, being yet unformed, and in your book they all were written. The days fashioned for me when as yet there were none of them.

Your Arms Are Open

THE MOST BEAUTIFUL AS A precious ingredient your arms are open wide both night and day, sough are the few born naturally gifted. Many faint in desire of what they would gain. I unveil my heart of transparent shades.

Adjusting to relationship is often a difficult process. It's fortunate you have made this course as smooth as possible from the sloop atmosphere with no substitute. Your substance are wonderful, often giving meaningful advice personally a reward to my life, giving eternal love and pride... how many time I rise having no regrets in my mind. You emulate the beauty happiness brought from the universe. Life is a story. Another mystery and we are the story teller. I am that man, that man that is good, born out of love, duration of my infinite soul. An oracle of ancient times within my mind, expanding my imagination of the cycle of life. I have discovered, before, and beyond, eon's of the immediate present, atom's ameliorating the unknown universe. A universe slowly expanding, earth scientifically shrinking, getting heavier in weight, failing natural life on a daily basis. Another mystery to man's minute mean's to indulge of answering overwhelming, unanswered, questions. With the choices, deadly reaction, and consequences. Maybe or not, two words I won't let defy my wisdom, knowledge, and understanding, "Praise Jah" Manifestations, of the heaven's and earth. Who fashion this day I have to live, live in a world in trouble. This I acknowledge. Though some may differ, not even assuming the same, denying the fact. But I know, that I know. Man is responsible, Jah give him dominion over everything, that is good.

Thank you for being who you are to me each day you are in my life showing me a special love and care, making me proud of your knowledge and understanding, being there in the moments when I needed you most. Thank you for everything mother.

Thank you for taking care of my cloths and keeping me clean, cooking me a descent meal, sure I was never hungry.

These are the reasons why I love so, you know me inside out, my do's, and my don'ts, my ups, and down, good and bad, you know when I am sick, or when I am happy and when I am sad. It's no wonder why I love you so you know when I am right, you know when I am wrong when I am telling lies or when I am telling the truth. You know that I want you to be in my life. You know that I am in love with you, there no wondering why you know me, you know I mean every word that I say.

Smiling Faces

YOUR BEST FRIEND IS YOUR worst enemy. I've seen all my eyes have allowed me to see and heard it all many times before in many different ways. Nobody is telling it anymore as it is what is real. Little do we know that so little has been done—a lot to lose, a lot to learn. The heart is deep. Destruction walks with smiling faces. Who knows what is in the heart of man? Sure you got a lot of friends and same amount of enemies. Who's counting? It's like a curse, underestimating petty, jealous friends you keep and have fun with. You don't know whom to trust. The questions I ask myself is: are poor men better than a liar? Is bread to the wise favor to the skilled? What if my friend is just a hypocrite? Can a lost friend ever be regained? Time may change this understanding, but I bet it would never cease. Good friends are those you cherish the opportunity to do the right things, bearing the responsibility. No if's, no buts, no maybe's, no in- betweens. My eyes have seen, ears have heard. There's a problem that urgently needs fixing.

The road to destruction is an easy one. The gates are open wide, but to walk the straight and narrow road and escape from hell to the upper air, this is when the trouble start.

Rejection Is Not A Good Fee

I HAVE BEEN TO NEW YORK, Mexico, and on the other side of the globe. Life is full of its usual disappointments, and rejection is not a good feeling, I know. I walk along the horizontal line, displaying a symbolic language. Attraction of the intelligence of the pen.

Wherever I go, this feeling goes. Sharing thoughts of my experience. I got to make some sense of change. The first thing I discovered was loyalty in question. Some will even push you down, though you have already fallen, but you call me your friend.

The mirror reflects yourselves. In this world, there are many secrets of the heart that goes deed down into the soul. Make a difference, having nothing to prove to anyone. Don't ever be ashamed, don't pretend. Everyone wants to be what they ain't.

In spite of all we face, it's my strong belief that each day is a brand new day. Be strong and confident. What we go through is everyone's reality. Look to the future in achieving direction and successful advice. Make all your visions come through, considering yourself a reliable human being.

You Got It

SOUGH ARE THE FEW THAT are born naturally gifted, still working hard doing what they love. Achieving their every gold they have set out to achieve. Many people has fainted, still in denial of what they would gain. Having no talent, to be skilled, too weak to be strong, and can't get it right. Inside out, upside down, all twisted. If you got it, you got it; if you don't, you just don't be the one fooling yourself, player, gifted, fronting. Play you all yourselves. I have got to be moving on to the highest heights with my feet on the ground and no time to waste. Life could be better for a change nothing to stop the way that I feel, love the vibes, and move with me. To the light let's do it together I have been around.

Sixteen Summers

SIXTEEN SUMMERS, A NEXT GENERATION with a lot of hopes and a lot of dream. Many stages, many changes. It's the world and times we are living in. Everyone in life has a part to play. What does it mean to be free here today to accomplish all our vision and goals? I hope everything will be all right. Things are gonna be okay. Somehow in our favor, whatever happens, that's the way it was supposed to be, but where do we go from here? Cherish all that we got, as we're still here alive to see another day. If we could only turn back the hands of time, we would bring back all those good memories if today hadn't faded away into yesterday and another day is gone.

Season has changed, years have passed, and summer is here all over again.

While we exist in uncertainty of the future, so are the children. In our children lies the responsibilities of tomorrow's sciences and technologies. Do we need peace or do we want war? What is the answer to the world situation today? Should we fight oppression and poverty once and for all, wipe them out from our minds with nuclear power threating our very existence and that could destroy every living thing off the face of planet earth? Our lives as we know it to be will never ever be the same. So remember to forgive so as to be forgiven. I do hope the Lord is going to answer all our prayers.

One day, as I was motion looking at things—things of creation—it occurred to me that all things with life appeared to be in motion, and it didn't matter how I looked at things. All life was driven by one thing—motion. Looking at creations, I get more out of life, and out of this came this understanding. It drew more out of me. All that life gave is free. What they mean to us is liberty. All through the day, the sun gives us heat; and at nights, the moon and stars shine brightly. When it rains, there's water, bird on the trees, fishes on the sea, and the dawn comes just before the morning. All life gives is free. What they mean to us is liberty through the ages within time, the element of life, and in the wisdom of creation.

Earth, wind, fire, and water, man has become one of God's creatures. And all life gives is free. What they mean to us is liberty. With his power, everything created is in motion beyond that, which shall come or would ever be seen or heard of. The past, present, and the future is blowing, and you will feel what you can't see is the gift of life and liberties in motion and give up the liberty we deserve. By the words "freedom and justice," you will be blowing and drifting away in the streams of your deeds.

Solid Grounds

DRY LAND, DRY LAND ON solid ground I stand. Seconds, minutes, days, weeks, months, years, there's no duration of time. Time doesn't stand still. There's only night and day. Of all that existed in the past, present, and future, all there is and all that we have is a limited system of measuring through the passages of lifetime. Light and space has no separation as well as the deep sea and the wide ocean. On every level, from the highest heights to the lowest, to the core, and to the foundation.

Unconquered

HOLDING IT DOWN, I WILL conquer them. Ready, willing, able, I rule my world. Gonna keep on moving, keep on stepping forward, and treading the earth. It don't matter what they say, don't matter what they try. Anything they do, they just can't win. What you sow, you shall reap. No negative vibes, be positive. What goes around comes around the same. Let me live and be free. You can plant corn and reap peas. Ready, willing, and able. I will conquer them. I rule my destiny. Keep on moving, stepping forward, treading the earth. Action speaks louder than words, mentally, spiritually, physically. They just can't win. What goes up comes down again. Ready, willing, and able, I will conquer them.

I Have to Live

WHEN IT RAIN, IT POURS. There's no one that answered to all the troubles that I face. Forgive me, judge me not, sorry is essential. Who is to be blame? I was worried all that I learned come. I thought I wouldn't make it through today. My emotion was getting the better of me. But consciously making my choices, at the end of the day, I have to live.

There's a purpose for me being here. In life, till death, and all the in- betweens. I am an ordinary man with every fault. If not life, what then?

Everyone has their part to play in the amazing events of life experiences. In this, I am grateful I am most valuable and honored to do all I can do for this world.

Withstanding the winds of emotional stress, executing positive manifestations here to accomplish all my dreams. Along life's journey, there's an unseen force by the order, and that might exist in creation that's keeping our feet on the ground.

At the same time everything is happening, the world keeps turning around all at once. As you're having strange dreams at nights, another life is born.

Gone is any reason why anything should be too strange for my mind. Lost, abandoned by the greedy, dying, my desires and broken promises, bad things I/we do in order to survive. With this, I shall not fail to meliorate my life, reminding myself that my mind is the instrument to raise me above my challenges. It's my moral responsibility and duty to the highest degree possible for tomorrow. Aware and prepared for today and for the future.

Sweet Peppers

CARROTS, ONIONS, CELERY, THYME, SCALLIONS, pumpkin, sweet peppers. You must have some of those sweet peppers to put in the pot. Can't do without them, those hard, green, juicy, bell-shaped, small, medium, large, yellow ones, and red ones. Sweet peppers from Mexico, the West Coast, Southern States, and the tropic islands. Sweet peppers in your Chinese, Indian, Japanese, Korean, West Indian, and Italian dishes. The flavor of those sweet peppers putting a touch of colorful to tasty, appetizing food in your plate. No cook should do without them. It is always a must in your favorite dishes.

One thing with those sweet peppers, they could be sliced into small slices, large, square, long, and thin in your chow mein. It's one of the best in terms of cooking. Pick up some at your favorite supermarket, at any corner of the Chinese or West Indian communities, and Korean markets in the vegetable sections. It's one of my favorite vegetables. I love cooking with those sweet peppers. I always have my refrigerator fully stacked, so you must pick up some. You would never want to run out. Keep some in your shelves. Pick up some of those juicy, sweet peppers.

How Could I Take You For Granted

PURPOSEFULLY, I SAT DOWN WITH enough time to think of you. Then I cleared my mind blank of any thoughts, letting it create in its own beauty of its craft. Knowing how life could be so uncertain, how could I take your love for granted?

I hope and pray with the understanding of God's wisdom. His idea of love inscribes my vision of you today, elevating my mind to understand the reason why you care.

Translating my experience into words that you can feel. Your love is a forceful inspiration that is eternally full and touched my heart. A source of fresh air. Giving me a good reason to value you in every way.

With your kindness and understanding, pass your positive attitude. Calming my nerves so easily. You clearly inspired my mind of the beauty of its craft, skillfully creating a special love for you in my heart and soul.

A Good Woman Is Hard To Find

THERE ARE MANY FISHES IN the ocean, billions of stars in the sky. By account, to date, a good woman is very hard to find. But for me it's okay. Allow me to demonstrate. I know your intention. Let me introduce you to yourself. You are inconsiderate, so inconsiderate that you don't care about anyone else's feeling but yourself. When you cry, you draw attention from everywhere else on yourself. Your needs are all that really matters. You are the most important and you are the core. Life must always center around you. You show no care, no compassion once the situation doesn't hurt you. The only feeling you care for is your own.

Other people's feelings just don't matter, and all you ever think about is yourself. There are good days and bad days, and each day are never the same. It's a perfect morning. Sunlight streaming through the windowpane.

Just as the first time I saw your face my eye's remained on you still to this day, warming up my heart. The right circumstances, I enjoyed it. It was cheerful to my mind. Your love is strong, making you who you are. Certainly making sure you are beautiful all the time, the morning have me thinking of you, holding on to that thought in perfect love all the way all through my life.

Other Side

NEW YORK, CHICAGO, CALIFORNIA, BIG cities all over the globe. What we go through everyday is reality and we are instinctively staying alive. Life is full of its usual disappointments and rejection. Where did our feelings go? Some will even push you down. Loyalty is in question. The heart goes deep into the soul.

As I walk along the horizontal line, there's a symbolic language, sharing thoughts of this experience. Intelligence got to make some sense of today. I discovered trust no man. Think we are not the same reflection of ourselves. To many secrets pretending to be smarter than average each his own potential enemy.

The forces are dangerous. Two forces, one weak and the other strong. Problems in all sizes, trouble without warning, whether guilty or innocent. They would try and take your life away. What have we done? Nothing, but the challenges that we face and the only element is the will to live until the dust is cleared and the rest could not be detailed. On solid grounds, I must stand.

Educate Yourself

EDUCATE YOURSELF TO THE HIGHEST degree. Use your intelligence to your fullest advantage, accumulate knowledge from modern time to ancient history, and visualize all the wealth you could achieve.

Days come and days go. Time waits on no one. Yesterday, you won't see anymore and I don't think you would ever again. I can't tell what does it mean. Today is here again.

Please talk to me tomorrow about today's reality. What have you done? Who is to judge? The truth must be revealed. So little answers to each question.

Lead is heavier than sand, steady looking at the hourglass. Along life's journey and in the events of your experience, have no doubts in what you believe. Turning despair into endless possibilities in the hopes of things not yet seen. Yes, faith conquers all fears.

Mandela

FROM HIS HEAD TO HIS toe, once place to the next. Storm fire of controversy. Life is full of its many disappointments and the times are dangerously unpredictable. You hoped where there was no hope, believed where there was nothing, but your philosophy has won you the victory. You'll live your life as a sacrifice with your love for liberty. But when you smile, it is the tool of you trade. Everything falls right into place, graceful, perfect, and complete.

The journey was never brief and smooth or without any interruption. Man pass are numbered like a fable story told. Forgiveness and renew good spirit to those lost, demoralized soul. With dignity and honor, the world bestowed upon you your right now, today. The one with iron will and endure resilience. Your spirit has displayed success, gently easing the yoke of inhumane injustice upon humanity. But when you smile, we rise from the depth of hellfire down below, ascending as the sun beaming upon the surface of the planet earth. You are the son no one could ever replace. It is a deep sense of human emotion, impossible to be contained. Your mind is the instrument of your destiny, your body is the temple of your wisdom, and your thoughts balance the negatives and positives to a higher spiritual degree; but when you smile, God is pleased with your happy face (Mandela). We sing and dance and generations shall clearly visualize we all must be freed. We are one big global family.

Who Am I? I am Man.

I AM PERFECTLY AND BEAUTIFULLY CREATED. The ultimate proof of bond to God by his word. The entire earth is my home. Citizen of the universe, who are you, I am. I am the visible and invisible element of life, positive and negative physical form. Manifestation brought forth by continuous reproduction. Who are you, I am.

Some people separate themselves from natural life. I exist only because of the other understanding. The indescribable beauty of creation and perplexity of God's divine power. Who are you, I am.

Wisdom is a scarce commodity. The mind is the instrument. With the proper use of the imagination, natural understanding would explain my experiences from past, present, and future. History will consider this true reality. Who are you, I am.

Evolution of the species is destructive in design. Thought-up inventions to complicate my mind. When logical facts and common sense is carefully applied to the use of understanding. Increasing the imaginative ideas becoming reality who are you. I am everything human. I am man.

Inner Voice

THERE'S AN INNER VOICE WITHIN me as long as time itself exist. Giving thanks and praises. Give thanks and praises for another day in time and another day in life. Remember, once a man and twice a child. But love is eternally here to stay. No one has ever been to heaven and back again and tell the story or the purpose for life.

No one on earth has ever felt my pain. It don't matter, I am sure I have been through hell. Once a man, and twice a child.

Knowledge is the principle thing. Season change, so do flaws; colors fade, and so do men. Let the strong show some humanity and help the weak. Who knows why we fight, who knows what the day would bring. But life is for living, and if you're not living, then you're dead. There's no tomorrow ever again.

LOVE CRIES BUT NEVER in vain. Love is a fire not even water can quench. Love is tender, as it's kind, an ocean that is never dry.

10/29/09

I envision in time when we will achieve that most wonderful gift where everyone is doing their best, making the world a much better place. Sharing love together will save our souls, and we won't cry anymore.

I PRAY FOR STRENGTH and honestly plead for life. Turning shadows into sunshine, and tears into smiles. A wealth of your tender-hearted support, making me the one who won your heart.

10/29/09

I will never hesitate instinctively presenting my love to you. When I shall resolve to seek your hugs, lay my head upon your breast, and to be folded in your loving arms again. Heart beating closer to better days. I am more in love with you.

I LOVE TO WRITE to you, taking you to the highest level of my love. Words so smooth, they are perfect in every way. Words that you can cherish.

7/7/09

Sometimes, I wish I could write, sit down, and look into your eyes as I watch your face bloom, while amazing you with my contiguous words that you become the most content woman, healing your ache and pain.

Hoping you would feel the sensation in your soul. I have a thing for you that I can't let go, taking you to the level of ecstasy, have you feeling good because of the beautiful things that I say to you are all true.

WHAT LOVE REQUIRES IS permanent. All other love is useless or worse. Maneuvers for short-ranged comfort. My love for you is with preexisting loyalty and faith. I know that much love is real friendship.

7/7/09

I have searched for that understanding so that I wouldn't mistake just passing through for permanent love. Let me introduce you to permanent love. Permanent love is not done in disloyalty, permanently justified.

7/4/07

Over and over in rhythm and symbol, personifying cheerful colors of the universe, twinkling lights, moon, and stars. Catch my pounding heart in the unconscious aspect of my love for you.

Your worth is more to me that a thousand words could ever express. All good things in my world in the spiritual and physical.

Thoughts beyond my fantasies, adding sweetness to my life, nothing to sour all my days.

Mama, I Am Gonna Make You Proud

FOR THE REST OF YOUR life till you're old and gray, Mama, in honor of you I am going to make you proud. You are a warm and gentle lady. You are my adorable queen. There are no words to depict your sweet, loving cake. Words are inadequate to defy what you truly mean to me. Your love never ceased or faded. You are a beacon of light throughout my life. No telling of with time will do for your happiness, but never cease or fade.

Mama, if anything should ever happen to you (Jah forbid), I will cry, shed tears in my room, my heart will ache and break with pain, and I will not be able to contain my emotions. Now that you are down in age, Ma, may God bless you both night and day, wherever you may be, good day every day for the rest of your life.

8/16/07

Sit down in the shade. Have some raisin cakes or fruits to your taste with great delight. Winter have passed, the rain is over and gone. Flowers are blooming, appearing on the land. A time for joy, celebrations, sunny smiles, and lots of fun. Birds are singing all over the land. Every day would be a good day for the rest of your life wherever you are. May you be blessed. Let love guide and protect you day and night.

Sit Down In The Shade

SIT DOWN IN THE SHADE, have some raisin cakes, and fruits to your taste with great delights. Winter has passed, the rain is over and gone, flowers are blooming and appearing on the land, birds are singing. It's time for joyous celebrations, sunny smiles, and lots of fun. You are patient, kind-hearted, and sweet. You are a warm and gentle lady. You are my adorable queen. There is no word to depict your loving care and what your love truly means to me. Words are inadequate. Light-years I will still doing my best for your happiness.

You are a beacon of light to me throughout my lifetime. Your love has never ceased to fade. Mama, if anything should ever happen to you (Jah forbid), I will cry, shed tears in my room, my heart will break with pain, and I would not be able to contain my emotions. You shine me a light where I could see into tomorrow. The uncertainty of yesterday no more exist. Mom, thank you.

I was searching wildly for love. I was so silly, like love was far away in distant places. Your love is a quality of perfection, making my dignity deserve respect, a compliment holding us together. It's powerful that I fall into a calm sleep.

6/1/09

My love for you will never be abusive, selfish in attitude, in competition, or in conflict. My purpose is to occupy a unique place in your heart, adding satisfaction and happiness to your life.

2/7/05

If there's any gap that remains between us that seems to be widening and has deepened, a stronger love is demanding to close that gap, more urgently now than ever before.

We both would see the closer we would come in achieving a more ideal love. It is more obvious it remains desperately in the event that rapidly changed both of us that would put a new focus in the way in which we think.

The true meaning of love makes our bonding more urgent to the extent that we can successfully resolve our relationship and hope to make better decisions day by day.

Family

FAMILY IS THE FABRIC OF our survival. Doing nothing, absolutely nothing, turned out to be the ultimate interest. Don't throw your life away not even contributing anything to family and the world. Lay a groundwork for the future. Make today better, keep an open mind, do not be surprised of anything. Allow one generation to fulfill and the others will sure to follow through. Education is the pillar of flaming fire for a better today. Some haven, some don't, and some won't.

Dear Dad

DEAR DAD, YOUR LOVE SHOULD never be any different from Mom. Your love should be exactly the same. You are responsible for every fiber of my existence, although Mom carried me and bore the pain. Don't ever try and act different in any sort of way.

A child needs both parents in nurturing and getting them ready for the future. But more seriously, depend on your action as a father today. In a world full of predators, what a child needs most desperately is a protector and a reliable source of security.

I love you in this moment that we share. I am expressing these feeling from my heart. You are the ultimate Dad, you are my hero, you make me proud, and you never let me down. From the day I was born, I relied on your love, encouragement, and support. Knowing who you are and what you want me to be, I am fully aware of the sacrifices you have made, emulating what a father should be. Now, I must continue this journey. Dad, I thank you.

On Solid Ground, I Stand

LIFE IS A CONTINUOUS CYCLE. On solid ground, I stand moving on and on. Through the passage of time, all we have is a limited system. The universe is open wide, no depths, no heights, time and space, darkness and light. Venus, Earth, Jupiter is in alignment, drinking from the fountain of love. Why do they call me? A man, unseen atoms formed in the rain, an illusion to your imagination. I am everything, no separation, no duration, everything that you see in existence, visible and invisible forms. Sunlight, rain, I am everything, a continuous cycle. Why do they call me a man? I am an illusion to your imagination.

Pineally Is The Keyhole

PINEAL IS THE KEYHOLE I view the world through unobserved, sometimes amazed sometimes amused. People keep me ticking.

Some people love to talk. A liar is known by his many words. Words without action bears no meaning and no weight.

Agree to not agree, each one teaches one that there is a lot more to listening and enduring to increase in our learning. Put away pride and arrogance, ambiguous and selfish opinion, and dictating the open mind. I discovered to trust no one. Think we are the same reflection of ourselves. As I walk along the horizon line, there is a symbolic language not spoken but shared in thoughts.

Determined To Live My Own Life

IWAS FREE WITH MANY CHOICES and lots of desires. I was determined to live my own life. I wondered far away off. My life was corralled, my own flesh and blood, also my so-called close friends denied me any comforting advice. What have I done? Why should I care? Who has given me instructions? Who was the judge? Lead is heavier than sand, steady looking at the hourglass. What does it mean to be free?

A poor man is better than a liar, so is a living dog than a dead lion. Even those without any objective deserve their fair chance. Bread is not to the wise, favor is not to the skilled. No riches to those with understanding but time and chance could happen to anyone.

Opportunity, I hope, will allow you to think and ask the correct question. It is essential to those who are career-motivated, but with opportunity come as much greater responsibility to show how grateful you truly are could be immensely rewarding.

Pray to the Lord so that he may offer you his friendship in the hopes of things not yet seen. Turn senseless choices and desires into endless possibilities, gaining fountains of water. Daily prospering in his knowledge. He will walk with you all the way home.

Convicted As A Team

MY BODY IS DEPRIVING ITSELF of all substance prepared for the slopes of uncertainty. I heard a gate behind me shut. I was trying to legitimately analyze what had transpired, convicted as a teen. I found myself in this tragedy, attempting to forge any mental scope of escaping a victim of society. With limited academic skills, a felon, under privilege, most likely will never succeed.

Broken in spirit, no future, my soul was growing wary of conviction. Who will take care of my family? I wondered. Accent to the bore of this misery. No door ahead. All doors behind me were shut. Solitude was my only sense of security. The bright orange setting sun calms my mind and put me at ease.

Time to think about making changes. I am free to turn around to a brand new vision. My mind is strong as a mountain, feet as fast as hindfeet, and thoughts contain atoms of intelligence. Uninterrupted memories were the better part of the day.

Be Yourself

I AM A BIG INTERNATIONAL SUPERSTAR through the ages. How often so many has made false, obscene, and ridiculous claims that hold no basis on facts and no merits bearing on legitimacy. In all the great accomplishment, which has been achieved, the most important of your gifts is your human ingenuity, which would turn out to be a beautiful, life-changing adventure. End to end shall meet and the cycle will continue. As one ends, another begins. No one knows how it started, but exceptionally, it's a unique skill. Discover your strength and conquer your fears. Reach for the stars, don't be egotistic, and don't get carried away. Just be yourself.

Be Yourself

NOTHING IS PERFECT. YOU, ME, life, death, black, white, big job, small job, king, queen. There is always going to be some unexplained, complicated circumstances. Folding challenges are never as simple as you would think. It is the same way in which one view themselves. It is the same way in which they shall be looked upon. You alone should defy your own authenticity.

There are multiple examples. Perform at your best. Confidence could be contiguous. Magical, no myths—though many may disagree—work hard, and make progress. Darkness, real fears, and danger is clear night and day. As many would agree, in the abundance of knowledge, she lives in many ways and only one time to die. The fool is crazy. The right to choose or not to choose is the free will. No two days are never ever the same. You could give a horse water, but you cannot force it to drink—one concept that should absolutely never change. Just be yourself.

Be Yourself

THE BEST ANYONE COULD BE any one verses all. They could never be what they ain't. Be real, and do not confuse yourself acting out those dreams. Quit while you are still ahead. It is a tendercy disappointing, immensely dangerous, and often offensive. Stop pretending. Telling tales won't help. Come clean, for only you alone is able to choose your own destiny, who you are, and what you want to be. It is not impossible. The honorable thing depends on your ability to conquer that scheme. The heart of man is deep. Someone who knows how things are done, the world cannot do without. Just be yourself.

Life Experiences Cannot Be Contained

THE ONE WHO THOUGHT OF the first diploma had none of his own books were made from common sense. How valuable are their contents. It took Common sense to write books, but the knowledge of life experiences cannot be contained. Refrain from all the negativity. Refrain yourself from uncertainty. It's taking too much time out of your day. Resist the monster greed that has done some dirty deeds. That mythical God held up his lightning rods, wanting to have all pity and petty causes. Tame the vicious beast. Don't hate. Why condemn yourself? Don't judge. Pursue your goals with intense passion, and take nothing away. Time is insignificant. The art of patience is a skill.

Tomorrow is getting closer, but the past could never be reset. Everyone deserves their fair chance in the pursuit of happiness. But if you are searching for tomorrow, I assure you that you are so late. At dawn, night has turn into day. As the glorious sunrise is over the horizon, the early birds come to sing songs of praises. When happiness is your ultimate dream, you don't need a certificate. Achieve happiness today.

You never see tomorrow, but it doesn't mean tomorrow do not exist. The arrow of time is blowing the four winds of destiny. Swiftly, shitting through both night and day. Celestial bodies, order, and the motion of the stars. Cherish them all at once. No one knows what the day ahead may bring. Your journey shall be full of special treasures and great rewards. There is no turning back. The falling rain forms, coming down from the limitless skies where you will find springs of living water renewing all precious life.

Words

I WISH WORDS HAD THE CAPACITY to convey my most silent, deepest inner thoughts, stimulating every molecule in my body. They would inscribe to the excellence of duty and sacrifice, love and joy. Sadly, they would fail to fulfill their vision of usefulness. Words, they just don't get it. Too simple to capture the act of kindness of the moment. I felt it. I did not know what to expect. Never were there anything to move me to instant emotion. Words, they are inadequate.

Reality of the trade winds blowing words of conflict, which will soon put us on a collusion course. Words and the irony of time, which advances us, is the one thing able to bring us to our demise. Some find the indifference shown by the privileged few are not so easy to accept, so they show no sort of emotion, don't even care to laugh or cry, live or die, consider disdain. The journey is just as import as the destiny.

The destiny is just as important as the journey. One moment we were celebrating, and another surrounded by the sorrows of saying our last goodbye, whispering if they would only explain how as the sun goes down. The universe fills the night of bright, twinkling stars. When a star dies, a new one is born again—perhaps to shine again greater lights on a future of infinite possibilities from the explosion.

From ancient man to modern times, words has played their part as a sort of inspiration to mankind. They never cease to empress us. We write words to the songs we sing; play music; once there is silence, wishes and dreams; and the shade that would oppose different sides of life. Words, in a huge universe where we are just a small connection of a continuous cycle of repeatedly successive succession, transporting the soul to different levels of consciousness. Growing up fast so quick, gone to early in their innocence. Full of life short-lived. Words, they are too simple, inadequate, and not showing what we are really feeling are the sorrows of uncertainty we experience each day. Words have their usefulness and meaning.

The Act of Communicating

WORDS AND COMMUNICATION IS AN art and one of mankind greatest discoveries. Some of man's most important accomplishments were through the art of communicating. To author the spoken words is a powerful gift. It is significant in order to convey intent while amplifying sensitivity to others. As mere man with flaws and faults, right or wrong, we may not get it right the first time. A common experience we share sometimes is lost in translation, but we are breaking down barriers, making small steps toward progress. Whispering in the present of company would be candidly rude with high expectations upon the platform of truth. From the pink dawn of time, like a force of nature, take full responsibility for our actions and live with them.

Speech is the one thing that takes us above any known species. A little thank you, excuse me, and please. Ever heard any conversation that has gone bad, lacking substance, tasteless, or just empty noise? Tame the tongue from twisted comments, speak when you are spoken to, and don't box yourself in as average, lowing your status and possibilities. Without good conversation, things would be so out of place. We all may fall into a pit.

Wait, I am not done yet. Take the first step with confidence. Help yourself. Man has his place in the past, conscious of the present, and journeying to the future, surrounded by mysteries with a purpose for being here. Mankind today is physically, mentally, and spiritually inspiring, so words are useful. Are they a force of nature or just an expression of speech? Each individual's voice has a different tone or sound.

Tomorrow

SEARCHING FOR TOMORROW LIKE IF it is just ahead of today. Looking forward to tomorrow, measuring time and space. Tomorrow is a trick. Pay attention before it disappears. Each day, tomorrow comes and leaves the same as almost yesterday. A.m. to p.m., a new day is here. What a difference a day makes. Now you see me, now you don't—tomorrow make quick exits.

Don't give up yet, and call it quits. Just because you have never seen a tomorrow doesn't mean it does not exist. I assure you, it is never too soon or too late. There will be another tomorrow, but don't leave to tomorrow what you could do today. The beauty about tomorrow is it could be any time, any day. And did it ever occur to you that tomorrow is just another day?

Sunday, Monday, Tuesday, Wednesday, Thursday, Friday, Saturday, seven days of the week. Tomorrow, where could it be? Where it should be, which is right in your head. Where else could it be? There are things eyes cannot perceive even when they are wide open. Procrastinating would not get it done. Peking would not determine a clear vision of this journey. You could search the whole year through, but tomorrow could never be found. Tomorrow is this moment and a promise to no one.

Where is the calendar tomorrow is written on? Is tomorrow a day, week, or month? Tomorrow is like a circle going round and round, gone before the break of dawn and at the rising sun. Like time, tomorrow waits on one as a canvass of possibilities in any new day of the year.

Winter, summer, autumn, and spring, only God knows what tomorrow will bring. Past, present, future, beginning, or end, tomorrow is only belated yesterday in the memories of today.

Unknown Destiny

THE CLOSER WE GET TO the moon with wits of mind that is penetrating distant birth of countless celestial bodies. Night and day, we cannot estimate light- years away where new civilization are born into concept, which also embraces life, so we journey to places of unknown destinies. Bizarre events and unanswered questions that throw the mind and spirit direct into deep myths and fantasies, understanding the world around us. Time is tickling out where we live, trying to explain how human existence came into manifestation.

Money Is Not A God

MONEY IS NOT A GOD. What they do for money, they keep on hunting it night and day. Money is not a God. Where is the honor? Brother is not a brother. Every day, I pray but not for money. My help comes from the Lord who made the heavens and the earth. Whatsoever I do shall surely prosper from this time and forever more.

Blood-thirsty men all fall from grace, truth, and the blessing. The righteous shall be saved, guided, and protected through these coming years. What is the difference from a boy to a man? There is no difference to the Lord between night and day.

Let the children, my family, relatives, and those who care for our well- being be granted wisdom, knowledge, and understanding that they may do the right thing. Their thing is money. It is all about money. Money is not a God. They would not do for the poor for Christ's sake. Today he is back again.

In a world full of deception and make-believes, all that they know are a lot of tricks. Some are afraid to wake up to the state of reality. I woke up this morning, and the beauty of my surroundings have captured me. Is it a fantasy? Was it a dream, illusion, or a mystery? Vertical, parallel, horizontal. What did I see? I could not believe what was happening today, like a force of nature was this reality.

Bird Songs, Calm Waters, and Bright Lights

Bird songs, calm waters, and bright lights, Bird songs, calm waters, and bright lights. Now, I have seen all my eyes allowed me, To see peace, love, joy, and happiness

Would you go wherever I go, or would you stay here all on your own? This I will never forget. This is my world bird songs, calm waters, and bright lights SLEEPERS, AWAKE FROM YOUR SLEEP. Love is a fire that burns from within. All will benefit. We have nothing to loose. This is the age of the twenty-first century. Look forward to the future, forget the war, and hate nothing but 100 percent. And now that we know what to do with love, all we need is our hearts to grow love everywhere. Bird songs, calm waters, and bright lights.

Bound in time and space, great mysteries orbit before the Genesis. Mysteries on journey to places of unknown destiny, spiritual mysteries that penetrate distance, and birth of countless celestial bodies. Mysteries to whom or what do we owe our human existence. Mysteries, bizarre events, and unanswered question that throw the mind and spirit direct into deep myth and fantasy. Mysteries to understand the world around us and where we live. Time will stop ticking trying to explain how these mysteries came into manifestation. The more we question the origin of life, it remain just what it is—a mystery.

The sun return precisely each morning, signaling the start of a brand new day. Closer to the moon with wits of mind. Night and day cannot estimate light-years where new civilizations are born into concept, which also embraces life, in fact stimulating critical sense relating to how we view ourselves. A question of when our own modern beliefs are question that consoling words may follow through by actions.

Finally, when will religion bring us a world of peace, love, joy, and happiness? What preventive measures are we willing to take, quantifying and calculating the judgment of the human race? Who is to blame when the little child speaks the yes of God? Negative opinion shall make a mighty noise when great minds stop their religious obstruction. The opportunity still remains in the mysteries that exist, bound in time and space, blowing out there with the winds of time.

There may be multiple reasons for our existence, but one concept should absolutely never ever change. The right to choose or not to choose is the free will. No two days are never ever exactly the same. The reason for life could not be accurately dated or explained. Nothing is new under the sun. Each day in life is full of mysteries, experiences, and discoveries that seemed too impossible to be explained. Just a lot of its life is a serious experience harder to explain. What is the distance between space and time? How deep is deep? How high is high? Why do the call was men, unseen atoms forms the rain only time would tell. Transcending past, present, and future.

Life comes in many forms so to is a higher degree of spiritual awareness. I adhere to proof, evidence, and fact and not stories. There is a reason and a purpose for everything that you see in existence. The ultimate beauty that is visibly and invisibly existing in nature, cosmic celestial wonders, the manifestation of life transporting the soul to different levels of sub atomic particles, bird song, calm waters, bright lights, joy, peace, and happiness.

The spiritual evolution of the soul ascended with the morning sunrise, shining bright with peace. The ultimate reality (figuratively or literally), light, and destiny were preordained, so to achieve the truth would never be a hopeless cause to the restoration of the future. Where wisdom, knowledge, and understanding are immensely rewarded, life secrets lies with God and not men. Life is truly a blessing to those who possess it. The dead know not that they are dead, and the unborn will never see the glorious, rising sun. In that moment, they parish. They knew absolutely nothing at all, but the living should know. When the balance of patience, tolerance, and understanding is achieved, people come together.

Peace is possible. No illusions to imaginative ideas. When the universe is at play, anything is possible, born absolutely, uniquely exceptional, and outstanding. You belong here, you belong here, you belong here!

The Universe

PAST, PRESENT, AND FUTURE, THE sun will rise in the east at morning time and sets in the west at evening time. The universe is a place of wonders and infinite space. Any given moment, the planets are in motion, as with time, held in place by the gravity of the sun. How magnificent the universe operates. Certain things were meant to be without subject to change, but life not operating on the simple, not-too-ordinary life is a bit more strange. Some people separate themselves from natural life, like a leaf flowing down the river stream. The fact that we don't understand the purpose of a thing does not mean it has no value. The evidence is significantly clear. All life is valuable, beautifully created, the ultimate proof, singularity, one kind. With heart's desire of need for peace as sunlight to all living thing on this planet earth. Man's senses must function to invoke clear works that express the vision of our experience, translating great thoughts into imaginative ideas, which will truly be an amazing achievement.

I understand wisdom is a scarce commodity. The mind is the instrument, and the body is the temple. Common sense, when carefully applied to the use of our natural logic, commonsense and understanding would explain our unique journey.

Evolution of species is destructive in design. Frankly, it is too confusing. The debate is over. Too many unanswered questions, which cannot be dated of its originality of life, death, and beyond invisible. Cellular molecules forms positive and negative elements, and the indescribable beauty of creation that evades the eyes that one cannot explain its complexities or celestials powers. Love has found you a course to lead you on your way home.

Happiness is a State of Mind

HAPPINESS IS A STATE OF mind. When you are happy, it's contiguous. You could see the signs, and everyone around you frees themselves of their sad state of mind. Life is a given. We had absolutely no hand in that miracle. Be thankful you were granted the gift of life to see another day, to see the glorious rising sun. Give back to life, giving to all things is the beauty and splendor forever of life would never be complete.

Be happy with doing the right thing the first time, so you won't have to do it all over again. A little at a time will make a big difference. At the end of the cause, happiness does not come with a manual recipe or script. Anything is possible. Where there is life, there is hope, passion, and the will to win.

Happiness is anything you put your mind to, and it is achievable only if you try to not give into your fears even if what you are confronting cause you to use all your wits. Great challenges in your work never ends, but incredible people does incredible things. Starting with today, look forward to the future. Life could change in a blink of an eye.

Happy to be a part of this human race, living in love to heaven and back again. Maybe we will sing and dance all the way, satisfied with everything and ourselves and no tears.

Share in other's heartaches and pain. Heal the hurt they feel. Happy that the earth keeps on turning under our feet, and we are not even aware of it. The heat of the sun gives us heat so we won't freeze, and water—precious water to life— to quench our thirst. Air we breathe must be fresh and clean. We need to live. We don't need to be wealthy and famous or show a certificate to achieve happiness.

You Had Your Fun

THIS IS NOT THE TIME for secrets. You had your fun, now those days are over. There is no place for regrets. Children of the future, I urge you to participate. Obstacles are there to remind us of the color of our skin. African and Africans at home and away abroad, it is not hard to remember, as it is easier to forget. It doesn't matter who you are, where you came from, where you are heading. The memories of the past must not linger on in our minds. No man is an island, no man stands alone, when our solution is already safe secured and sealed.

All are created equal in the eyes of the creator. No one is inferior, no one is superior, and to no one, brotherly love is the highest. Let us address these following. I know they would like us to cool their heels, but we are not servants. Nobody are slaves or their property. With all my inalienable right, I'm emulating all the greatness man has ever achieved, acknowledging my moral duty. Human beings has the responsibility to love each, and every human being owe. I am a free man. Don't call me a nigger boy! Africa shall rise on top of the world. We have been down too long for 4,000 years, separated, killing our free soldiers, fighting for nation, unity, liberty, and strength. Unto us a child is given, unto us a child is born. I see the rainbow, and I know it's a sign.

HOW YOU KNOW WHAT I mean many times, do we have to fall and rise, fall and rise again hating ourselves we paid the price, many time had to bash our heads against a wall, come go with me for the ride, together around the red, gold and green. A leopard, cannot change it spots? Can a tiger change it stripes? Morally, a black man could never ever be white don't even matter how hard he may try. Don't put off the rainbow tomorrow may just be too late, Africa, and Africans must be free as proud people, right away. Beautiful Africa is the place where we love to live in the cradle of creation, where there is plenty of food and space generations shall grow up healthy and be free Africa.

Born on a Wednesday

I HAD NOTHING TO DO WITH it. I did not ask for it. It was in the middle of the nineteenth century when it began, or that is what they said. Born on a Wednesday, I open my eyes to the light of day. Was I here before? When did it begin? How will it end? Am I sun? Am I a moon or one of the earth's creation? Fantasy or reality? Dream or a mystery? One thing serves the other and other serve the next. Were all the things in life connected through a nature process of time or was it immediate intervention? More question that answers no answers to the questions I ask. Years now, I have been here. There must be a reason why the sun shines, why the moon comes out at night, and the earth is full of life. What an amazing and beautiful place. I am water, I am the wind, I am one of the sources of all entire story without end. This is what I will begin with. Who, what are the reasons why, and where did it start. Never mind, it is a blessed gift. I won't mention any names because for you and me it is the same thing.

Balance the Pendulum

TO HIDE THE TRUTH IS a specialty hidden by negative authority. Even more deadly when it wears the cloak of familiarity. The skeptic say our thoughts are on a lost cause. My world is colorful with the sun in the morning, moon and stars at nights. A world, which is self explanatory, no hidden secrets, guess work, no luck, or chance. I am a part of everything that make me one.

The other side of darkness is a light of valid questions that are unanswered, unheeded, disguised, and surrounded by mysteries of cosmic energies. The spoken word when bang. What happened next was good and enlightening to all. The universe. There is a power flowing through our veins it cannot be silent, calm, or tame. You receive what you give. Attracting negative, positive balancing the pendulum.

Till The Earth

TILL THE EARTH RISES, SO as I open my eyes, I am satisfied. Let thunder roll, lightning strike, most cherish beauty splendor shine. Till the earth rise in honor, power, and grace, mystic majesty, and take your rightful place. Let all eyes look toward the east and see, rise, run high, strong and full of might, swiftly, westerly heat circulating point to point over land, home, earth, and sea.

Till the earth rise with time on your side, let it be known to all eternity. Till the earth, ten thousand years, ten thousand times. Ten thousand lifetimes throughout the ages, forever in existence. Till the earth, magnificent nature, and essential sustenance gift to humanity. Till the earth, immediate intervention, master of all intelligent designs, born of a natural birth. Till the earth, pinpoint accurately clear, precise answers are infinitely inaccurate. Till the earth, life, from the smallest to gigantic microorganism, cellular molecules, subatomic particles, stable to unstable forces of nature, extremely determined, domination of death vision of obscurity. Till the earth life, our most precious commodity. Treasure it.

Your best friend is your worse enemy. I have seen all that my eyes would allow me to see, heard it all many times before in many different ways, and no one tell it as it is. What is real of the little that we know? So little has been done, a lot to loose, and much more to learn. The heart of man is in deep destruction, walks with smiling faces. Who knows what is in the heart of men? Sure we got a lot of friends, same amount of enemies, but who is counting anyway? It is like a curse underestimating petty jealousy. Friends you keep and friends you loose. Friends you have fun with, but you don't know if whom to trust. Questions I ask myself: what if my best friend was a hypocrite? Can a lost friend ever be regained? Time may clear up this understanding, but I bet it could never change. Good friends are those you would cherish to the opportunity to do the right thing. No ifs, no buts, no in between. There is a problem that urgently needs fiddling.

She is The Womb Of The DNA

SHE IS THE AGCT, DOUBLE helix code of life, living organism, womb of the DNA. She is a paradox of the milky way of time. She is a mystery of the cosmic galaxy, the blue planet of our solar system. The strangest I have ever seen. Genius, incredible, brilliant, pretty good strategist, more than we could ever explain, see, hear, smell, or feel no straight lines, no empty space. Are you ready and prepared to be amaze, listen to the songs of her wild atmosphere? Energy fields, electromagnetism, gravity, microorganisms, bacteria, cellular molecule, subatomic particles.

What goes up must come down, what goes around comes around again. Winter, summer, autumn, spring, time and season's cycle change. Positive, negative, cause, and effect. Lightning, thunder, storm, and hail. Oh dear, while the other planets are either too hot or too cold, and they are totally inhospitable. From her womb, diversification of species is revolutionary leaps of nature. Rain forest, deserts, waterfalls, birds, fishes, trees, sun, moon, stars, man, and even the animals also give her praise. The most complicated I have ever seen. Magnificent, extraordinary, efficient, and pretty good strategist. More than we could ever explain. No straight line, no empty space, not yet amazed, she sustains all living things. She is a goldilocks, a gem, a jewel, pretty little glowing Cinderella. No straight lines and no empty space. Listen to the songs of the wild environment, snowcapped mountains, bright moonbeams, blue skies, green grass, bountiful harvest, river streams, natural wonders, site for all to see, her gifts, and masterpiece.

She has known each of us for a very long time and made everyone feel happy. By taking good care of us, she have been taken for granted. Why would you want to destroy the only place you are sure that life truly exist, which would be damaging to our future. Through ages, our relationship has been at a critical stage when it should have grown stronger. She is a constant giver, reproductive to the good and bad and at times very unforgiving, awesome, powerful, majestic, and most of all, the beautiful place we call home. Mama nature, we love you our darling sweet earth. A love that withstands the test of time is the greatest love for life. The fruit of the womb is a mother's reward (womb of the mother of all living things.)

There's More to Life

IF A LION REFUSES TO hunt, is he still the king of the beast? If a river runs dry, is it still a river? There are more to life on this journey. Like a beautiful song, ice crystal palace of the arctic, dewdrops on the cactus of the Andes Desert, crickets distantly chirping in the silence of the night, stars up above looking down on the darkness of the night, spring of living water renewing all precious life. Some things are meant to be discovered and better if were left alone, unknown.

Don't throw all that is known away. Shine your light where you can see a better day. The eye, which is the window to the soul, could not get pass the beauty it beheld. Tomorrow and the uncertainty of yesterdays will soon disappear. The person you are is trapped on the inside. Truth is what you feel in your heart, logic is completely exhausted, and it is too impossible for knowledge to explain what is woven into the fabric of our existence. A special favor may bring back great rewards, but there is much more than enough when love is involved. How could you find love outside oneself if you cannot find love from within? It is clear that it is not negotiable, frankly unnecessary. Make it be specific. Only you could make your world be a colorful world and your day a beautiful day.

Lift up your spirit, I am a proud, black woman with the mind of a winner, philosophy, and determination. I am like music, sweet music, melody and harmony, good sound to your ear, a light to the entire household. I will bring joy to your heart, morning, noon, and night, and peace over and over again. I will be your song for all times. I am always in your world.

Apart From You

MY PLEASANT WAYS ARE UNPARALLEL qualities to embrace. I will be your fresh air on the surface where oceans are deep. Rest at the seashore like a flock of bird in pairs. Beauty is endangered and looks cannot last, virtue would cease, but my radiance never fades.

My heart is like a burning flame, a passion that can't be silenced, clammed, or tamed. Perfection of love expands the universe. Treat me good, and the favor will be returned. Springtime, harvest, and earth are my friends; children are my most wonderful gift, so as snowcapped mountain and bright moonbeams. I am a symbol of fertility, always bright and clear.

One hundred percent, three sixty degrees, I am a queen in all history. I populated this planet this great human race, builder of nations with no comparison, black dignity. Give me due credit in the proper way. I am woman, there's no other in this world like, black queen. Red, Gold, Green.

Apart from you, everything else is so hard to bear—one big mess. But you being in my life, my thoughts of you are very special ones. All I ever get from you is pure love time after time. Again, as long as I live, I see the goodness in you that give me comfort and hope all the way. You have done your duties well forever, and I will carry you in my heart, determined to do my best through the coming years.

You are a warm and gentle lady, my adorable queen. There is no speech to depict, for words are inadequate to defy what your loving care mean to me. Showing me that love truly never cease, and is patient, kind-hearted, and sweet.

You are a beacon of light throughout my life, and I will do everything to secure your happiness. If anything should ever happen to you (God forbid), my heart would ache and break into pieces. I would also cry, shed my room full of sadness and pain. Mom, in honor of you, I am going to make you proud. The fruits of the womb is a mother's reward.

The sun gives us light and heat all through the day, the moon and stars shine at night, and when the rain falls, there is water. Birds for the tree, fishes for the seas, and the dawn come just before the morning.

Nefertiti

NEFERTITI, THE BEAUTIFUL ONE, HAS come. You appear at dawn, bright as the sun in the morning. Your name is like perfume, and hair is like waterfalls. You are a beautiful rose in a garden that fill my heart with joy. Let me kiss you on your lips. Honey is under your tongue.

Now, when I look around, it somehow came to me this understanding of the liberty that you gave me, lifting me up from all angles, drawing my attention by showing me special care. You ravish my heart with that looks in your eyes. How better is your love than spices and wines? The links of your necklace and the scent of your perfume sweeten our love. The fragrance of your garments is like the fragrance of Lebanon.

I am proud through these stages that within time, all the elements of life, earth, wind, fire, water, and all God creatures has become inspired by you, Nefertiti, Egyptian Queen of the Nile.

To you, when I love, I feel rather than think. My vision has put my faith in your love to this reality. Offering truth in my character, constituting my love for you. I present my art product to you alone, urging you to claim that what I purpose here is true. Therefore, my love cannot be trampled under or, by any means, die. My love for you would be everlasting.

I thought I was loosing you, but I was only loosing my grip. I thought I had control that made me walk away. I took an intelligent look at the worse thing that I ever did, to my regret. I know now that I should have stayed. The life I chose to live was no better. I had to make a change, my thoughts were of you today, and I must now admit that I thought of things that never even exist.

Every time we touched, my heart felt the object of your love in a not so perfect world. With you, there is an extraordinary closeness that exist between us that it is not too hard to imagine the infinite ways, which solidifies our love.

There are two things that I could imagine that could outshine our brilliance: the difference of species in nature and intricate cut of rough diamonds. Based on these two combinations that bond us together, I now put on your finger this ring.

I walk through the dusty trail into the illusive door of our existence, no limits to my experience to relate between reason, truth, and consideration. Each day, I wonder isn't love more than we could ever imagine? Be moved by our emotions. Love is a very special thing. There is no mystery that cannot be resolved.

Love is Substance

WHAT IS LOVE? LOVE DO exist, as reindeers, ducks, and butterflies. Love is wild, first mate, soul mate, love at first sight. Love is substance. A powerful source of nature that fills our hearts with joy.

Love comes in many faces, shades, and shapes. Love is all we preciously embrace. Many need a little bit of love today. When the world delivers love, whoever receives it is amazed in profound depth of what true love really mean. When love is nowhere to be found, we could never ever be free of a lonesome soul. Love is a mysterious beginning with many swirls, curls, curves, and bents. Love is sharp, shaping into a rapid flow that brings survival to cities. None shall escape the mighty power of love. Love is the highest, curving quietly into a ceremony, celebrating harmless, and peaceful as a dove. Love is high up in the mountains and even out in the open fields. Love holds no fears and it conquers all things.

The wide-open ocean and the deep, blue seas. A jealous spring and envious lakes, angry and dangerous. Love folds to no foe. Love is a powerful source, like a great river that rule or ruin our lives. Love is a bit of everything when added to what matters to us. Somehow, it is better like rosemary and coconut oil.

Adjusting to New Relationship

ADJUSTING TO A NEW RELATIONSHIP is often a difficult process. It is a fact and the evidence is clear. Scarcely have I found love. One could never be too certain. Joy has turned aside, replaced by selfishness. Indulgence, obscured vision lead by the mere light of day.

Fortunately, you have made this course as smooth as possible from the slopes to the upper atmosphere. Sough are the few who are born naturally gifted, giving new meaning and desires to what we have now achieved.

No stranger thing would ever happen to touch my heart and the eternal qualities you have shone. My heart's transparent shade unveiled. Your substance is wonderful, a most precious ingredient adding to your beauty brought from the universe. Together, both of us will explain the operation of love, and the fact that loves comes in pairs. But we, being mirror images of each other, which make us one, is never too strange to my mind.

Consequently, so many are searching and trying to find their piece in their missing puzzle. To date, all searches have turned up unsuccessful except, for the record, our love would be exceptionally unduplicated. The magnetic force between us cannot be proven wrong but it has already been accepted the fact that love comes in pairs.

Speak Up

TELL ME I AM GOOD; tell me I am bad. Speak up and tell me about us, whether it make me happy or if it make me sad. Don't tell me what I want to hear because it won't be fair. I dare you to challenge or to doubt my love. I dare you. With iron and steal, cold as ice scorpion's stings, serpent blood, and poisonous bites, lethal danger to my life.

I love you as the morning, winter, autumn, and spring. It got to be love all year through. At sunrise to sunset, day in and day out, as time and seasons change.

Tell me to hold on, or if I should let go, speak up. Tell me what you love. Tell me what you hate. Express your inner emotions, and don't hesitate. I dare you as your beauty fill my soul like arrow through my heart, like daylight sunshine up so bright, as candles calmly lit the night. My love is good and not bad, and it safe and strong. Love is always the same, surely doing what is right. A life of blessing is a struggle you won't ever have to face. It cannot be anything else. It got to be love or the aftereffects would only hurt and pain.

Tell me in your own word. Tell me the honest truth. Speak up and tell me what I mean to you in your heart. I need to know. I dare you. Moon shine bright while predators storks and while shepherds herd their flocks. Come live with me forever.

More Hours than Time

MORE HOURS THAN TIME TRYING not to remember the past, which cannot be reset but could have been better. Our love is the present, anticipating the future. The more love grows, it will always keep us together.

Many people are together, many people say that they are in love, experiencing positive connections, emotions, and signs, but they are not sure. Every time one walk through the door, the other is insecure. I thought I was in same category. It had been said that all men are dogs, but baby, when I told you that I love you, it was from the bottom of my heart. You are my past, present, and future and the one I truly adore. Life is a story and we are the storytellers.

My caring must have made it necessary and sufficient condition to love you. My caring must have been intelligent enough, adding to my capacity to know you. To receive love, to give love, and to be loved, we will comfort each other.

Some people grow old and have lived still not knowing what to do. But we love knowing we will always be together, keeping us together. Love of this kind will multiply in all the appropriate areas.

Insecurity I/Daring

I dare you to challenge or to ever doubt my love. I dare you with iron and steal, cold as ice, serpent blood, and poison bites, lethal danger to my life.

> I dare you, as your beauty fill my soul,
>
> Cupid's arrow through my heart by daylight sunshine up so bright.
>
> As candles calmly lit the night.
>
> I dare you. Come, moon, shine bright while shepherds heard their flocks, predators stork.
>
> Come live with me forever.

JUST IN TIME, SHE shines like Venus bright in the morning sky, as she always do. Her pleasant thinking is an unparalleled quality as a treasure we embrace. Unconscious to that fact, those are the things that set you apart from the best. A princess always handles her business professionally. As her presence fill the room, what a difference the fragrance of her perfume makes as it circulates in the atmosphere. Without pretense just right to be the person, you are correct.

What we have here between us will outlast generations. Through the passage of time, no one can tell the future, but a new chapter lies ahead. We have weathered every thunderous storms, confronted many forces, deceit, jealousy, and frustration. Elements which could destroy our union. What we have here took patience and understanding. No script, recipe, or manual book to guide. Relationship comes, relationship goes, parting days, weary way, fading signs, and distances. This one will outlast throughout time immemorial.

ZION IS A HOLY place, and no sin shall enter therein. What is a tree without roots? A dead tree. What is faith without works? No faith. What is works without faith? No works. Some has chosen not to submit to grace. They had to flee and run away. Time is running out, no time to waste. I must take the first step, leading over the mountaintop till I reach over on the other side. Lord, send me help, hear me in my prayers, cherish my heart and thoughts, and help this union grow with confidence. You are the shepherd; I am the sheep.

Beyond the distant horizon where mere man had never been, where sin shall never intervene, your name is inevitable above the most beautiful sunrise. Higher than all the excellence and wonders of the universe. Time could not display the power and the glory of your name.

Fact merits legitimacy. There are three forces among us: active, positive, and negative. Each day, there is an atomic struggle to balance the weight of the fall out, wearing down on us. This is the message:

Don't get angry

Don't be afraid

Don't complain

Don't wait too late

Don't be violent

Don't cheat or trick

Don't do them no more

Don't say them no more

Don't go there no more

Do them with authority

Or this:

Life would be worth absolutely nothing at all. Don't be mad. Sour grapes would only cause your teeth to edge. And we are north vertical. Look up and not down. There are infinite possibilities with the universal stars.